Invention of Facebook and Internet Privacy

A MODERN PERSPECTIVES BOOK

Tamra B. Orr

Published in the United States of America by Cherry Lake Publishing
Ann Arbor, Michigan
www.cherrylakepublishing.com

Content Adviser: Satta Sarmah Hightower, Writer & Editor, Talented Tenth Media, Boston, MA
Reading Adviser: Marla Conn MS, Ed., Literacy specialist, Read-Ability, Inc.

Photo Credits: © Rawpixel.com / Shutterstock.com, cover, 1, 19; © sturti / iStock.com, 4, 10; ©Rick Friedman/Corbis/Getty Images, 5; © michaeljung / Shutterstock.com, 7; © janniswerner / iStock.com, 9; ©shironosov / iStock.com, 11; © Rena Schild / Shutterstock.com, 12; © wx-bradwang / iStock.com, 14; © FLDphotos / iStock.com, 15; © RayaHristova / iStock.com, 17; © bombuscreative / iStock.com, 20; © PeopleImages / iStock.com, 22; © arek_malang / Shutterstock.com, 23; © Sipa via AP Images, 25; © digitallife / Alamy Stock Photo, 27; © Alexey Boldin / Shutterstock.com, 30

Graphic Element Credits: ©RoyStudioEU/Shutterstock.com, back cover, front cover, multiple interior pages; ©queezz/Shutterstock.com, back cover, front cover, multiple interior pages

Library of Congress Cataloging-in-Publication Data has been filed and is available at catalog.loc.gov

Cherry Lake Publishing would like to acknowledge the work of
The Partnership for 21st Century Skills. Please visit *www.p21.org*
for more information.

Printed in the United States of America
Corporate Graphics

Table of Contents

In this book, you will read three different perspectives about the invention of Facebook in February 2004. While these characters are fictionalized, each perspective is based on real things that happened to real people during and after the invention. As you'll see, the same event can look different depending on one's point of view.

Chapter 1

Jonathan Villani

Harvard Junior

I sat down at the desk in my college dorm room and stared at my name on the computer screen in front of me. There it was: Jonathan Villani, my own personal profile on TheFacebook.com. It was awesome. I had just gotten started **uploading** information on it. So far, I had listed my name and basic contact info.

"Hey, Ben," I called to my roommate. "Look at this! We can even rate our professors on here!"

Ben leaned in over my shoulder. "Cool! What else can you do?"

I wish I knew. I should have listened more closely when Mark Zuckerberg was talking to his friends about the program in computer

▲ *Mark Zuckerberg only attended Harvard University for two years before dropping out to run Facebook.*

science class. At first I thought he was talking about some science-fiction novel he was reading. Then I realized he was describing a real Web site he had created for all of the students at Harvard University. I should have known he was serious. This was the same guy who had invented the CourseMatch and Facemash programs earlier. That last one had gotten him in big trouble, too—something about using photographs without permission.

TheFacebook.com was something else, though. Facemash had focused on deciding who the most attractive girls on campus were. I had to admit it had been fun comparing two photographs and choosing between them. Too bad the Web page was shut down before

Second Source

▶ Find a second source that describes what's on a current Facebook page. Compare the information there to the description of the original Facebook page.

▲ *The Facemash program used student photos without having permission from those students.*

Think About It

▶ Read the paragraph about the short-lived
Facemash. Why do you think it was shut down
so quickly? Give two reasons why you think this.

it was even 24 hours old. I had heard Zuckerberg say that he was
really surprised it had caused so much trouble.

CourseMatch had been about choosing which classes to take for
any given college major. You could see who else would be in your
class, which made it easier to take the same classes as your buddies.
On the other hand, TheFacebook was about staying in touch with
everyone at Harvard. You could send a message to your friends. You
could ask a general question or find out what was happening on
campus that weekend. I overheard Zuckerberg say he had **launched**
the site four days ago, and now there were already more than 650
profiles posted on it. Maybe my profile was number 651.

"This site sure beats those facebooks the school hands out each
year," Ben said. He was right. The **directories** Harvard distributed

were nice. They featured the names and pictures of students and were supposed to help us all get to know each other. However, they certainly weren't as much fun as this online version.

"Jonathan, just imagine what we might be able to do with these profiles," said Ben. "Maybe we will eventually be able to post photos or start study groups."

▲ *Nearly 22,000 students attend Harvard University each year.*

▲ *In 2004, there were only 1 million Facebook users.*

"If the faculty added profiles, we could communicate directly with professors, too," I replied. "Maybe one day we could share music with friends as well."

"Or find out more about some of the girls in the other houses," Ben added with a grin.

I went back to uploading information for my profile. My relationship status? Definitely single. Looking for? New friends, of course. Interests? Reading, hiking, video games, and graphic novels. "I'm almost done," I said to Ben. "Now, I'll just add my birthday, e-mail address, and cell phone number, and it will be complete."

▲ *Facebook was originally used to help students stay in touch with friends at Harvard University.*

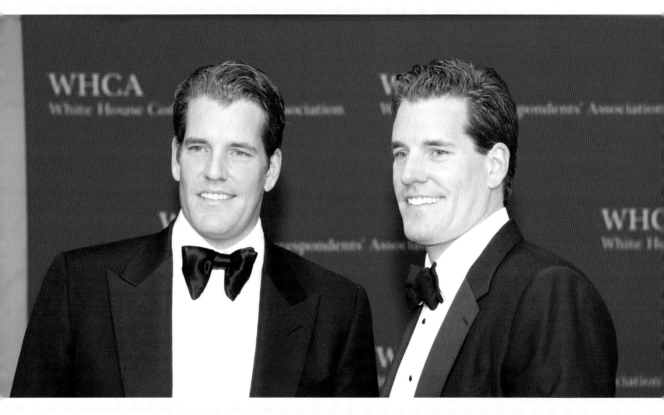

▲ *The Winklevoss twins attended Harvard at the same time as Mark Zuckerberg.*

Ben frowned. "Wait a minute," he said. "Aren't you worried about putting all of that personal information out there for the rest of campus to see?"

I paused and then shook my head. "Nope," I replied. "It's just other Harvard students. Why should I worry?"

Who Owns an Idea?

Mark Zuckerberg is fully credited with coming up with the concept of Facebook. But twins Cameron and Tyler Winklevoss believe he stole the original idea from them when all of them were attending Harvard. The twins sued Zuckerberg for $65 million and settled out of court in 2008.

Chapter 2
Olivia Connors
Harvard Professor

"Well, Zuckerberg has done it again, Olivia!" Professor Edmonds said to me as I walked past his office.

Oh no—not another Facemash, I thought. What an embarrassment that had been. "Now what?" I asked. "We're not back to that silly 'hot or not?' situation, are we?"

Edmonds shook his head. "Thank goodness, no."

We both clearly remembered last October when the Web site Facemash had been available to Harvard students for a single day. In a matter of hours, 450 students had visited the site and voted more

▲ *Mark Zuckerberg started Facebook with friends Chris Hughes, Andrew McCollum, Dustin Moskovitz, and Eduardo Saverin.*

than 22,000 times on the pictures of women they had found there! Facemash had quickly resulted in outraged letters from several groups on campus, including Fuerza Latina and the Association of Black Harvard Women. Zuckerberg was called in front of the school's Administrative Board a few weeks later. Both Edmonds and I had been there to hear the **accusations** against the young man and then to help determine his punishment.

"Mr. Zuckerberg, you are officially accused of **breaching** security, **violating copyrights**, and violating individual privacy with this Web site," the student was told by the Ad Board. He had **hacked** into the databases of nine of the school's dorms to get the

Second Source

▶ Find a second source that explains what a copyright is. Compare that information to what Mark Zuckerberg did when he created Facemash. What did he do wrong?

students' photos. Then he had uploaded them onto Facemash. In addition to stealing the photos, he had not gotten permission from anyone to use their pictures.

Zuckerberg had defended himself by saying that he was fascinated by the science of creating a program like Facemash. He stated that he had never intended to hurt anyone's feelings or insult

▲ *After the disaster of Facemash, Facebook took user privacy seriously.*

anyone or break any school rules. Although we all discussed
suspending or **expelling** the young man from Harvard, in the end,
we decided to put him on **probation** and ordered him to see a
counselor. He also was required to send letters of apology to the two
women's groups he had offended.

"So what is the latest from our dear Mr. Zuckerberg?" I asked
Edmonds.

"It's something called The Facebook."

"Like the directories we give out?" I asked. Edmonds waved me
over and showed me one of the site's profiles. I had to admit, it looked

fun and much more entertaining than the facebooks we handed out. But when I spotted all the personal information students were posting online, I felt a ripple of concern.

"Look at this," I said, pointing at the screen. "It lists each person's birthday, e-mail address, and cell phone number. Those are a lot of personal details. Is that safe?"

Professor Edmonds shook his head slowly. "I doubt it," he said. "My guess is that Zuckerberg isn't too worried about it either."

As I walked into my office, I couldn't stop thinking about TheFacebook.com. My guess was that it would work like a dream for

▲ *Users post 510,000 comments to Facebook every 60 seconds.*

▲ *Today, people use Facebook on their computers, cell phones, and tablets.*

our students and they would love it. I just hoped the Web site would not prove to be a security nightmare for everyone. As long as the site is restricted to the Harvard campus, I decided, everything will work out safely.

Fascinating Facebook Facts

Active users (July 2016)	1.71 billion
New users added every day	500,000
Average amount of time spent on Facebook per day by users	20 minutes
"Likes" generated per minute on Facebook	4 million
Number of photos uploaded each day to Facebook	350 million

Chapter 3

Lucas Thompson

Potential Investor

"**H**ey, Sullivan, have you heard about TheFacebook.com yet?" I asked my business partner.

"Is that a new dating site?" he replied.

"Not quite. It's not about meeting people. From what I've seen, it's just about keeping in touch with family and friends," I explained. "It started at Harvard University. Within a month, it had gotten 10,000 users, and it just kept growing. Within a couple of months, half of Harvard was using the site, and now it is being used throughout Stanford, Columbia, and Yale."

▲ *Facebook spread across campuses by word of mouth.*

Think About It

▶ Read the paragraph about the people who worked with Zuckerberg. What is the main point? Pick out two pieces of evidence that support the main point.

"Really?" I could tell from Sullivan's arched eyebrows that I had caught his interest. "Is it like that new site, MySpace?"

"Yes," I replied, "but this one seems to be spreading far faster. I read the other day that Peter Thiel just invested money in the site."

"The guy who founded PayPal?" Sullivan asked. "That's impressive. Who is behind TheFacebook site?"

"Some young computer genius named Mark Zuckerberg," I said. "Of course, he had help. His roommate, Dustin Moskovitz, helped him with the technical end of things. Two others students, Chris Hughes and Eduardo Saverin also contributed. Hughes acted as the spokesperson for the site. Saverin managed the finances and networked with potential advertisers. Andrew McCollum helped out

▲ Peter Thiel was one of the original investors in Facebook.

Moneymaker

From being a cofounder of PayPal to investing $500,000 in the early days of Facebook, Peter Thiel has made some very smart decisions over the years about where to put his money. By 2016, this graduate of Stanford University was worth more than $2.7 billion. Today, he is involved in SpaceX, the rocket-building company, and a data analysis company called Palantir.

with the **graphic design** aspect of the site. Together these guys have developed something pretty unique."

"How does the Web site make money?" asked Sullivan. "Do you have to pay to have a profile on TheFacebook?"

"I wondered about that, too, and did some research. Being on TheFacebook does not cost anything at all," I replied. "Advertisers pay to put their ads on the pages. With thousands of people checking their

▲ *Today, most companies have Facebook pages and advertise to users on Facebook.*

Second Source

▶ Find a second source that confirms Zuckerberg was approached by Google. Compare the information there to the information here.

pages every day—some of them every hour or more—those ads are seen a tremendous amount! Imagine what could happen if those thousands became millions. Then imagine if Zuckerberg could find a way to tailor ads to reflect people's preferences and interests. I think this could be a potential gold mine."

"Have the guys run into any serious issues yet?"

"Actually, yes. They had to redo their site awhile back to limit the personal details that people were putting on their profiles. It was causing a real security risk because too much private information was being shared with the entire Internet," I explained. "Other than that, all they have done is grow."

Sullivan pulled out a chair and straddled it. "So—are you thinking of investing in this?"

"I am," I admitted. "I called Zuckerberg the other day. He told me that he was recently approached by a New York investor who wanted to buy TheFacebook for $10 million. He actually turned the guy down. Rumor has it that Google even made an offer, and Zuckerberg said no to that one, too."

I could tell Sullivan was growing increasingly interested.

"I think the site has real potential," I continued. "The cost of running it is almost nonexistent."

"Good point. There is no big warehouse to pay for, no customer service department to staff, and no huge **inventory** to keep stocked." Sullivan paused to think for a moment. "We need to do some real homework, Lucas," he finally said.

"You're absolutely right, partner. Let's start by creating a profile and see what we can find out about TheFacebook. Then, if it looks good, let's run this by the board next week and see what they think."

Look, Look Again

Take a close look at this Facebook timeline photo. Use the image to help you answer the questions below:

1. How do you think an original user of TheFacebook would feel about the new features of Facebook?

2. What do you think a professor concerned about privacy might think about the things users share on Facebook?

3. What would someone who had invested early in Facebook think about the numbers of people who use the site today?

Glossary

accusations (ak-yuh-ZAY-shuhnz) the charges made against someone for doing bad things

breaching (BREECH-ing) breaking a law or agreement

copyrights (KAH-pee-rites) the legal rights to control the use of things created, such as pictures and music

directories (duh-REK-tur-eez) books of names

expelling (ik-SPEL-ing) forcing a student to leave school

graphic design (GRAF-ik dih-ZINE) using art and words to produce a book, magazine, or Web site

hacked (HAKD) to secretly get information from a computer without permission

inventory (IN-vuhn-tor-ee) a stock of goods

launched (LAWNCHD) got something started or introduced something new

probation (proh-BAY-shuhn) a period of time that tests someone's ability to improve or behave well

suspending (suh-SPEND-ing) temporarily having a student leave school

uploading (UHP-lohd-ing) transferring data to a computer

violating (VYE-uh-late-ing) disturbing or invading without any right to

Learn More

Further Reading

Cornell, Kari. *Facebook Founder and Internet Entrepreneur Mark Zuckerberg*. Minneapolis: Lerner Publications, 2016.

Dobinick, Susan. *Mark Zuckerberg and Facebook*. New York: Rosen Publishing, 2013.

Harris, Ashley Rae. *Facebook: The Company and Its Founders*. Minneapolis: ABDO Publishing Company, 2012.

Lusted, Marcia Amidon. *Mark Zuckerberg: Facebook Creator*. Minneapolis: ABDO Publishing Company, 2012.

Mattern, Joanne. *Facebook*. Minneapolis: ABDO Publishing Company, 2016.

Web Sites

Kinooze News and Facts—What Is Facebook?
http://kinooze.com/what-is-facebook

Minor Monitor—Facebook Safety for Kids
www.minormonitor.com/resource/facebook-safety-for-kids

Index

About the Author

Tamra Orr watched all of her kids sign up for Facebook, and in 2010 finally gave in and signed up, too. She enjoys the Web site and checks it daily. She is the author of hundreds of books for readers of all ages. She lives in the Pacific Northwest with her family and spends all of her free time writing letters, reading books, and going camping. She graduated from Ball State University with a degree in English and education and believes she has the best job in the world. It gives her the chance to keep learning all about the world and the people in it.